Adventures with
JONNY

Let's Go Fishing!

A parent and child fishing adventure and guide

Michael DiLorenzo

Illustrated By Jenniffer Julich

Running Moose Publications, Inc.
Clinton Township, Michigan

Printed in Singapore

Published by Running Moose Publications, Inc.
42400 Garfield Road
Clinton Township, MI 48038

Publisher's Cataloguing-in-Publication Data
DiLorenzo, Michael A.

Adventures with Jonny: let's go fishing! – Clinton Township, MI: Running Moose Publications, 2006.

p.; cm.
ISBN: 0-9777210-0-0
ISBN13: 978-0-9777210-0-9

1. Fishing. 2. Fishing-Handbooks, manuals, etc. 3. Fishing-Equipment and supplies. I. Title.

SH439 .D55 2005
799.12-dc22   2005911198

Book production and coordination by Jenkins Group
www.BookPublishing.com

Cover and interior illustrations by Jenniffer Julich
Layout by Eric Tufford

Printed in Singapore
10 09 08 07 06 • 5 4 3 2 1

This book is dedicated to my son, Jon...

...who is my inspiration and my tireless fishing buddy.

To my daughters and part-time fishergals Mikelle and Kailey, you gals rock!

To my father, who took the time to introduce me to the world of fishing at the ripe old age of three and hence planted the seed that would grow into a lifelong passion.

To my friends, who taught me a thing or two about fishing along the way, or just endured all the fishless campaigns as we cut our teeth on this wonderful sport.

To the students and teachers of Hugger Elementary School in Rochester Hills, MI, for their time and input in helping me to create Jonny.

And finally, to my wife, Laura, who has tolerated many a spousal absence, yet still sends me off with a smile as I pursue my outdoor passions. Her support has been vital in bringing Jonny and the series to creation.

Why did I create Jonny?

The writing of this book, the development of Jonny, and the basis of the Adventures with Jonny series is to introduce young children to outdoor adventures that can become a key part of their lives to be enjoyed forever. If you as a parent can give your child the gift of the outdoors, you will give him or her a gift for life.

The pace of today's society, the burden of too many structured youth activities, and the ravenous consumption of our children's time by television, video games, and computers denies them the opportunity to experience all that awaits them in the world of outdoor pursuits. To run without a coach, to play without instruction, and to learn without a lesson plan are but a few of the many benefits that outdoor adventures can provide to our children.

I hope that more families will once again grasp the value of the outdoor experience and recognize the traditions that can be built together around regular outdoor adventures.

The outdoor experiences you share together will no doubt create some of your fondest memories and establish themselves as building blocks of your parent/child relationship, as they have done for my family and me.

Please enjoy this book with your children, and take them fishing when you're done.

Fish on!

Photo by Keith Jasukaitis

Table of Contents

Jonny's Fishing Adventure

The moon is still shining when my dad comes to wake me

We're driving
to the lake
where we'll fish
for the day

We both are
so excited
we'll sing songs
along the way

4

I grab my tackle box
and my favorite fishing pole
My daddy takes my hand
as we walk to the fishing hole

5

It's early in
the morning
and I see
the sun rise

The lake is
so pretty
I can't believe
my eyes

6

Geese and ducks fly over
they honk and they quack
Just then we see a fish jump
and land with a smack

7

The birds are all up singing
the fisherman's morning song

Boy I am so happy
my dad took me along

8

We rig up our poles
and I pick out a worm
When you have one in your hand
it really likes to squirm

Since I am so little
I soon get the jitters

That's when I wander 'round
and start looking for some critters

11

I roll over some rocks

and I turn up a log

And that's where I find

a painted turtle and a frog

12

The rod is shaking in my hands
as the fish and I fight

And my dad keeps telling me
to keep the line tight

The fish is getting tired
so I pull him toward
the beach

A
few
more
turns of
the handle
and he'll be
within our reach

I get to hold my catch as my dad takes out the hook

Then I hold the fish away and take a really long look

19

Then my dad gets a fish
as he whistles a little tuney
But compared to my bass
his fish is kind of puny

22

We laugh and we talk
about other fishing places
I'd like my friends to come fishing
so there'd be more happy faces

The morning soon flies by
the rising sun gets really hot
So my dad says to me
"It's time to leave
this fishing spot"

24

Parents' "How-to" Fishing Guide
Adventure Tips for Parents
Getting Started on Your Adventure

So, you're going to introduce your child to the adventure of fishing. To help make your adventure fun and meaningful for both of you, here are some things to keep in mind:

Let's Get Excited

Get your child excited about your fishing adventure by reading fishing magazines together or taking a trip to your local sporting goods store prior to going on your adventure. What child can resist all the bright, colorful lures and mounted fish (which are often equally or more entertaining to the adults)? Have fun with the comical names manufacturers give their lures: Jitterbug, Tadpolly, Daredevles and Hot n' tots, just to name a few.

Learn Good Fishing Waters

Though all fish live in water, not all water holds fish. Check with your friends or others you know who are fishermen or go to your local tackle shop to find out exactly where to go and what to use to catch fish. If you are brand new to the sport, take a page from your children and ask lots of questions. All fishermen are novices at one point in their lives.

Fish When You Can

You don't need to wake up at the crack of dawn to catch fish. Let's not make this too uncomfortable for you or your little buddy: fishing can be just as good at noon as it is at six in the morning. Generally, fish tend to be more sluggish during the brightest time of day or in the heat of the day, so fishing may be better in the morning or evening. However, fish feeding habits are fickle and can change at a moment's notice. So, don't limit yourself to these times. Go fishing when you can.

Food and Water

Regardless of the adventure you are on, children are bottomless pits when it comes to food and drink. Bring along plenty of snacks and drinks, which not only will satisfy their endless appetites but will also help keep their minds busy between fish nibbles.

Be a Teacher

A child's initial introduction to fishing is very important. Try to entertain and educate your child with all that you are experiencing together while you are on your adventure, especially since fish are not always very cooperative. This helps take little fishermen's minds off the downtime between bites.

Beating the Boredom

So your little adventurer does not get bored, keep the first few outings short—unless the fish are in a feeding frenzy and are keeping you both pleasantly entertained. At the first signs of boredom, try talking about the nature that surrounds you or playing games. For example, you might try to identify all the wildlife you see on your fishing adventure.

Can We Talk?

Fishing also represents the golden opportunity to just plain have a conversation with your kids about life itself. You may be amazed at how much you can learn about your children and the experiences they are going through in life. In the hustle and bustle of today's world and with running kids to countless structured activities, we seldom get the chance to have an open-hearted conversation with them.

Celebrate!

While on your adventure, celebrate everything from a nibble to a successful retrieve of the line. Your child's cast that goes even remotely in the intended direction deserves at least a small barrage of high fives.

Say Cheese

When it all comes together and your little adventurer lands that first fish, celebrate the catch and preserve the moment with a picture. The look on your child's face at that moment cannot be duplicated later in the day. It is definitely worth holding onto. That first fish, regardless of size or species, is a trophy to your child and should be celebrated accordingly. Also, upon a fish's demise, it will quickly lose its color and be much less photogenic.

It's Not about You

If you're already an avid fishermen, then most of this simply may not apply. Still, try to avoid getting caught up in catching fish for yourself and thus leaving your child bored. Remember, this adventure is about introducing your child to the sport of fishing.

Don't Give Up

Your first adventure may not work out as planned, but do not lose enthusiasm or dampen your child's spirits. Fishing is truly an adventure, and the most unsuccessful trip can quickly turn into a trophy experience. You never know when the fish may suddenly decide that the worms you're using are the tastiest snacks they've ever had.

Safety: the Most Important Reminder

Last, but certainly not least, is SAFETY!! I have purposely left this item for last so that you remember it first. Whether your adventure takes you on a boat, pond, river, or lake, please always have your child wear a proper-fitting life jacket. Seeing you wear one will also help sell the idea to your child.

Target Species

Since the object of your adventure will be to successfully introduce your child to fishing, this book will target the most cooperative and abundant of all species, the pan fish. This family of fish includes bluegill, sunfish, rock bass, and perch and requires minimal initial investment to get outfitted for your adventure. The concepts and basic techniques that we will discuss can be applied to other larger species as your child and you grow together in the sport of fishing.

What Do I Need to Get Started?

Fishing Licenses and Rules

Most states require that adults have a fishing license, even when just fishing with a child. Along with your license, you will receive a complimentary rule book from your state's department of natural resources that will inform you as to what species of fish you can legally fish for at the time of year you are embarking on your adventure, how big the fish must be in order to keep it, and how many you can keep should you and your fishing partner have a good day. In most states, minor children do not need a license to fish but must be with a licensed adult and must abide by the same fishing rules and regulations that apply to adults. A fishing license can be picked up at most sporting good stores or tackle shops.

Fishing Poles

Fishing rods come in various flexibilities, referred to as actions, from ultralight to heavy, with many options in between. The lighter the rod, the more flexibility and sensitivity it offers. Each type of rod has a purpose. For smaller fish, use a light or an ultralight rod suited for the tackle you will be using. This helps children more easily feel the sensation of a small fish biting the bait, and they will have much more fun as the rod bucks and bends while they reel in their fish. Remember, the longer the rod, the more difficult it will be for a child to handle, so keep to rods less than five feet in length. Fishing rods also come in different styles. Two of the most common are spinning and bait casting, and either could work for a good starter rod. However, for an easy introduction to fishing, I suggest using a lightweight bait-casting rod matched with a spin-casting reel, which brings us to the next topic of discussion. All fishing rods, regardless of model, indicate the action, compatible fishing line strengths, and rod length on the rod, just up from the handle.

Look for rod description to be printed here

29

Fishing Reels

Several models of reels are available, again each designed to do something a little different or for different-sized fish. Little children have little hands, and the focus of our efforts will be for them to catch smaller fish (those pan fish that I mentioned earlier). Thus, you'll want a little reel for them to use.

Spin-casting Reel

The model of reel best suited for introducing a child to fishing is the spin-casting or closed-face reel. It is the easiest to operate: your child simply pushes a button (the cast button) at the rear of the reel when beginning the cast and releases the button at the end of the cast as the rod swings in the desired direction. This reel also offers the least chance of line tangles, which can single-handedly frustrate the most patient of us. The closed-face reel would be matched with a bait-casting rod.

A second choice of reel would be a spinning or open-face reel, which would be paired with a spinning rod. As your child's knowledge grows in the adventure of fishing, this type of reel would be a well-suited step up, as it allows for different types of fishing that may require greater line capacity on the reel. Although a spinning reel is slightly more difficult to cast, your child could easily master the process with a bit of practice.

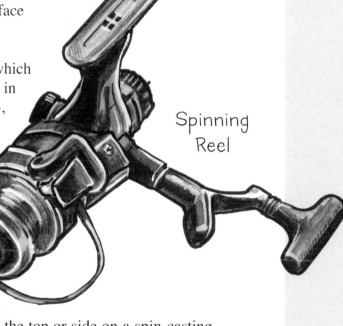

Spinning Reel

Fishing Reels - What a Drag!

All fishing reels have a drag, which on a spin-casting reel comes into play only when the cast button is locked back into its fish-ready position. This feature, controlled by an adjustable dial located on the top or side on a spin-casting reel, controls how much pressure must be applied to the line (such as when a fish pulls) before the reel releases the line. The drag should be adjusted so that moderate pressure on the line will allow it to pull from the reel without breaking. The drag control on a spinning reel is normally located at the front of the reel, though some models place the control at the rear of the reel.

Regardless of your reel selection, if the drag is set too loose, virtually any pressure or weight on the line at all will pull line from the reel and prevent your child from reeling the line back onto the reel. If the drag is set too tight, the line will not pull from the reel no matter how much pressure is applied to the line. In the case of too tight a drag setting, the line eventually will break, most likely when your child hooks that trophy fish that will quickly become one of the many mythical "fish that got away." The textbook setting for your drag is 50% of the pound test rating of your line. But, since no reels have a poundage rating indicator, just pull on the line with your hand to make sure the line does slip from the reel before reaching its breaking point. Whew! All this talk about drag is getting to be a drag!

Drag Tips

1. Do not reel against the drag. If your child is snagged or has hooked a big fish and they are not gaining any line as they reel, stop them from reeling until line can be gained on the reel again. The result of reeling against the drag is very twisted line that will tend to coil around the rod tip during future use and can be greatly weakened in the process.
2. Always check your drag setting at the beginning of each fishing adventure and throughout the day. Oftentimes, idle fingers get to playing with drags, and then in the moment of truth, the line may snap if the drag setting is a bit too tight.

Rod and Reel Combinations

Together, the rod and reel are referred to as combinations. You can purchase such rod and reel combinations already prepackaged and sporting the popular cartoon character of the time. But, I would forgo some of this packaging hype. The quality is often compromised for the sake of graphics, and the accompanying tackle will often be of little use to you and your child. However, some of these are high-quality, neat little combinations just the right size to start your son or daughter off on a fishing adventure. On the plus side, most of these combinations come prespooled with line, eliminating the sometimes frustrating task of loading line on the reel.

Fishing Line

Fishing lines, like their fishing rod counterparts, come in varying weights, referred to as pound test ratings. A pound test rating is the pressure point at which the line will break. Lines range from 1 pound to 100 pounds and all points in between. Fishing line is one of the most important items of your fishing gear. It connects your child to the fish. As fishing line ages, it becomes brittle and weak. Old fishing line will likely snap at the first hint of pressure or, more likely, when your child hooks his or her first fish. So you do not want to use the old fishing line that has been lying around the house since that science fair project five years ago.

For the sake of pan fish, four-pound test is ample for the job. Your child can cast lighter fishing line more easily, as it is quite limber and has much less tendency to coil up around the tip of the rod.

Just because your child has four-pound test fishing line on the reel does not mean he or she cannot land a five-pound fish. If your child hooks a large fish, loosen the drag slightly to relieve the pressure being put on the line while your child reels in the fish. It's okay if the fish pulls out line from the reel; this just adds to the fun of fighting the fish, and that's why we are here in the first place.

Loading Fishing Line onto Your Reel

To load fishing line onto your reel, regardless of the type of reel that you are using, first feed the fishing line through the eyelets of the rod, downward from the rod tip towards the reel. You can then follow the knot diagram illustrated below. As you complete the knot, trim the end of the line within one-eighth inch of the end knot, moisten the line, and draw the knot tight. See page 33 for step by step instructions on tying this knot, based on the model of reel that you are loading line onto.

Spin-casting Reel (Closed-Face)

1. Open the reel (unscrew the top) where the line feeds into the reel and place the line through the opening in the reel top, leaving the cover off the reel.
2. Place the line around the spool of the reel, taking the end of the line and tying a simple overhand knot around the main line. Draw this knot snug around the main line. Then tie a second overhand knot into the end of the fishing line. Clip the end of the fishing line within one-eighth inch of the end knot.
3. Moisten the knot and draw the main line tight. The knot at the end of the line will meet the main knot and then as you continue to pull, the line will cinch tightly around the reel.
4. Replace the cover on the reel, then reel in enough line so that the spool inside the reel is almost full.
   For this type of reel, it's best if someone else places a pencil through the spool of fishing line so that the line spins neatly off the spool and onto the reel. You may occasionally want to open the reel during the process to see how much line you have on the reel. Fill the spool to within one-eighth inch of the spool's edge. DO NOT OVERFILL THE SPOOL.
5. When the reel is full, cut the line from the filler spool and tie on a snap swivel using a palomar knot (see page 44) and clip snap swivel to any rod eyelet support to avoid line tangles.

Internal Spin
Casting Load

Note: keep a slight tension on the fishing line as you fill the reel so that it loads neatly on the reel and without any loops. You can do this by pinching the line with your fingers as you reel the line in or have gentle pressure applied to the spool of fishing line held on the pencil by your assistant.

Spinning Reel (Open-Face)

1. Flip open the bail of the reel.
2. Place the line around the spool of the reel, taking the end of the line and tying a simple overhand knot around the main line. Draw this knot snug around the main line. Then tie a second overhand knot into the end of the fishing line. Clip the end of the fishing line within one-eighth inch of the end knot.
3. Moisten the knot and draw the main line tight. The knot at the end of the line will meet the main knot and then as you continue to pull, the line will cinch tightly around the reel.
4. Flip over the bail and reel in enough line so that the spool is almost full.
   For this type of reel, lay the spool of line flat on the floor and reel in a small amount of line.

Spinning
Open Bail

33

If the line begins to twist, flip the spool over and continue to reel until the spool of the reel is full. Fill the spool to within one-eighth inch of the spool's edge. DO NOT OVERFILL THE SPOOL.

5. When the reel is full, cut the line from the filler spool and tie on a snap swivel using a palomar knot (see page 44) and clip snap swivel to any rod eyelet support to avoid line tangles.

Note: again, keep a slight tension on the fishing line by pinching the line between your fingers as you reel in order to neatly load the line on the reel and avoid any loops.

Tackle

Fishing tackle is a subject without boundaries! Every fisherman has a favorite hook or lure and will argue its worth to the ends of the earth. However, for the sake of your child's first fishing adventure, I am going to stick to hooks, weights, and bobbers.

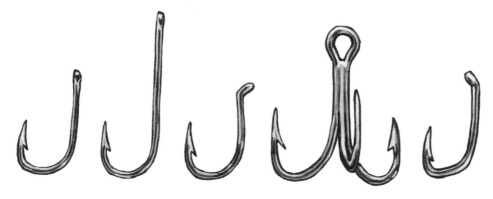

Hooks

Fishing hooks come in all different shapes and sizes, designed with varying bends and twists. One thing is for sure, they are all very sharp and should be left to the adults to handle during your son's or daughter's initial fishing adventures.

Try to get a hook that is right for the job at hand. If you are fishing for smaller fish, stick to smaller hooks. Many times I have witnessed fishermen going through worm after worm on their over-sized hooks without landing a fish. Well, unless Jaws swims by, chances are they won't catch anything. The majority of the fish will not get that giant hook into their little mouths where it needs to be to do its job.

Hook manufacturers use an even number system to identify the size of their hooks. This system relies on the logic of "the bigger the number, the smaller the hook." In general, for pan fishing, try to use hooks no wider than one-quarter of an inch from point to shank, about the width of a small paper clip. Depending on the hook manufacturer, sizes to use would be #8, #10, or #12 or you could look for the obvious package that says "pan fish" hooks.

You can purchase plain pre-tied hooks, hooks with fishing line tied directly to them with a loop at the other end that attaches to a clip tied to the end of your fishing line. These attached lines are called leaders. You can also buy hooks without leaders, so that you can tie them directly to your fishing line.

Hooks are inexpensive, so take plenty along on your adventure; kids have the uncanny ability to cast into every snag that lurks above and below the surface of the water. Before your first outing together, you may also wish to become very proficient in tying knots. If not, you will get plenty of practice during your fishing adventure!

Lures

Fishing lures come in as many variations as there are shoes for women, and fishermen, like women, can justify having limitless quantities of these.

Since you are just introducing your child to the basic concepts of fishing, we will keep the "lure speak" to a minimum. You can use a few simple lures once your child has mastered the basic casting and reeling skills.

Basic lure styles include spoons, spinners, and plugs. Any of these lures can simply be cast out by a child and reeled in at a slow to moderate pace. You'll find many different manufacturers and variations of these basic lure designs, and they range significantly in cost. Since lost tackle is part of the learning curve, let's keep the curve as flat as possible. Stick with the lower-cost tackle and watch the sales at your local sporting goods dealer or tackle shop.

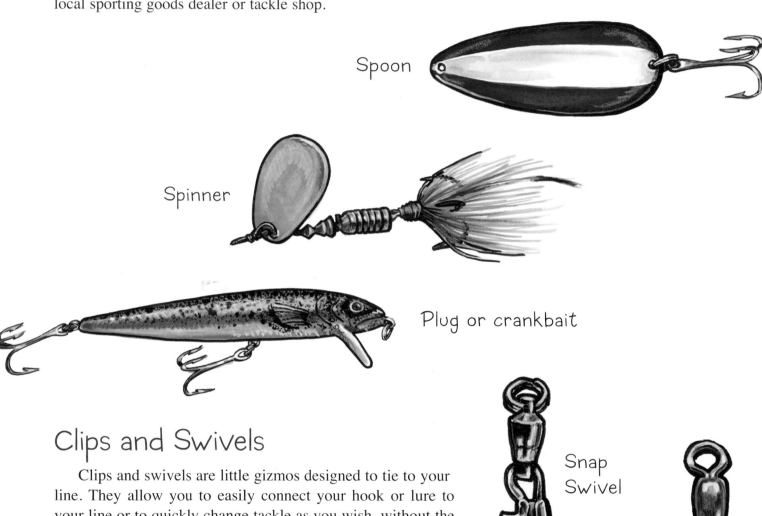

Spoon

Spinner

Plug or crankbait

Snap
Swivel

Swivel

Clips and Swivels

Clips and swivels are little gizmos designed to tie to your line. They allow you to easily connect your hook or lure to your line or to quickly change tackle as you wish, without the need to retie your line. They also help protect the fishing line from getting twisted as the line is being reeled in by your little adventurer. The more twist that gets into the fishing line, the more difficult casting will be. Also, a great amount of line twist can weaken the line.

Bobbers/Floats

Say "bobbers," and most people quickly think about the large, round, red and white plastic model. I suggest using stealth bobbers (see illustration) for one reason: they catch more fish. The large round bobbers make quite an announcement when they hit the water and can spook the fish in the area where you are fishing. Also, when a fish does bite the hook, the pencil shaped model offers much less resistance, which gives the fish less tendency to spit out the hook.

Traditional
Round Bobber

Stealth
Bobber

Weights

Fishing weights, commonly referred to as sinkers, come in a variety of weights and shapes based on the type of fishing you may be doing. You don't need to select weights that could double as a boat anchor. The more resistance a fish feels while biting your bait, the less interested it will be in continuing to bite. Use just enough weight to do the job at hand. Some sinkers have a small, built-in eyelet, allowing them to be clipped to your line. Other weights, referred to as split shots, look like small BBs; a cut in the center of each enables you to pinch the split shot onto the line. All of this will make sense to you once you start fishing with your child

Split
Shot

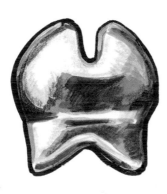

Sinker

Miscellaneous Adventure Items

An overwhelming number of trinkets, gadgets, and gizmos fill the shelves of most tackle shops. Some of these will eventually have a purpose as your child gains fishing skills, but many can result in impulse purchases that will have little or no use in your child's tackle collection. These are fisherman catchers but not fish catchers.

A few other key items to take on your fishing adventure would be:

a small tackle box that helps you keep fishing equipment sorted and easy to access

a small fishing net to scoop wiggling fish out of the water

a fish stringer or fish basket for keeping caught fish fresh by keeping them alive in the water until you and your adventurer are done fishing

a hook remover and hook removal pliers to allow you to reach the hook in a small fish's mouth and to aid in avoiding sharp teeth when removing the hook from a larger fish's mouth

a camera for taking pictures of your child's priceless adventure

a fishing log (notebook) to keep a written record of your memories

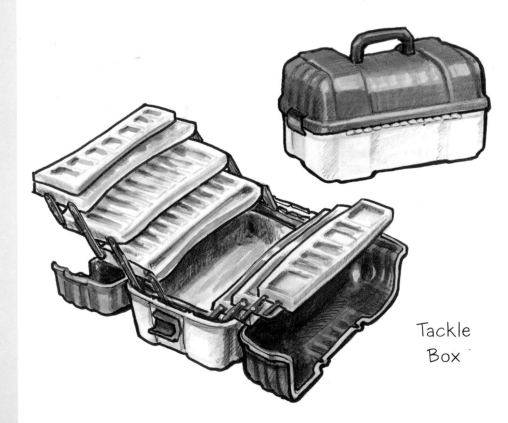

Tackle
Box

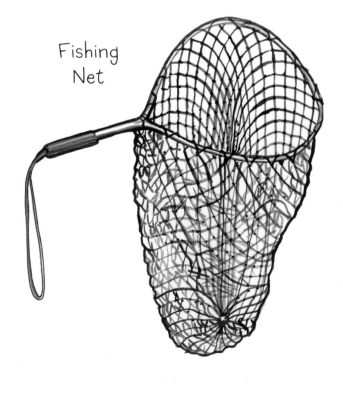

Fishing
Net

Fish
Stringer

Fish
Basket

Hook
Remover

Hook Removal Pliers

Fishing Log

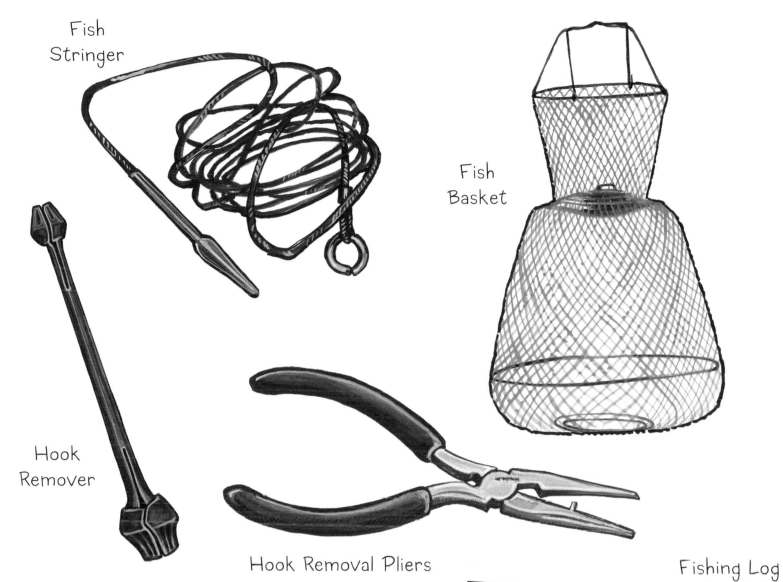

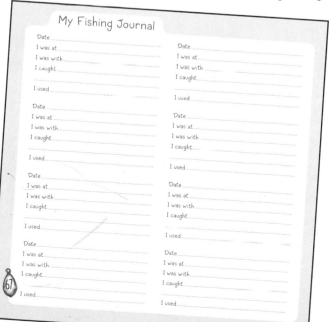

My Fishing Journal

Date
I was at
I was with
I caught

I used

Date
I was at
I was with
I caught

I used

Date
I was at
I was with
I caught

I used

Date
I was at
I was with
I caught

I used

Date
I was at
I was with
I caught

I used

Date
I was at
I was with
I caught

I used

67

Camera for taking pictures

38

A Bit of Casting Practice

Trying It at Home

Casting is a very simple process that can easily be learned by your child with a bit of practice at home prior to your first fishing adventure. Before your child begins casting hooks, try practicing with a small sinker or casting dummy tied to the end of the line.

How to Cast Spin-Casting Reels (Closed-Face)

Spin-casting reels have a large cast button at the rear of the reel. The fisherman pushes this button with his or her thumb to keep the line from unwinding too early. The button is released to allow line to freely spool out of the reel. The line will not release from the reel while the button is depressed. Only after the button is released will the line pull freely from the reel. To pop the button back out and stop the line from flowing from the reel, turn the crank or handle on the reel forward at least one full rotation. This is the fish-ready position.

To get children acquainted with their fishing poles, have them:

1. Clip a small sinker to the snap swivel at the end of the fishing line
2. Hold the rod directly out in front of them, parallel to the ground
3. Press and release the cast button so that the sinker will fall to the ground
4. Reel the line up so that the sinker is within one foot of the rod tip
5. Repeat this a few times to develop a feel for the action of the reel

Drag Control

Cast Button

Spin Cast Reel

Casting for Real

How to Cast a Spinning Reel (Open-Face)

As a reel on which to cut their teeth, the spinning reel is a bit trickier for small children but will most likely be their reel of choice as they grow into the sport.

The spinning reel has at its front a semicircle of heavy gauge wire, referred to as the bail. Locate the place where the bail meets the reel and there you will find a roller that the line rolls over as it is being retrieved. To cast a spinning reel:

1. Clip a small sinker to the snap swivel at the end of the fishing line.
2. Grasp the line with the index (pointer) finger, holding the line in the first crease of that finger. Do not hold the line against the rod.
3. Flip the bail over with the opposite hand until it locks into the open position.
4. Release the line from the finger by stretching out the finger and allowing the sinker to fall to the ground.
5. After casting the line, return the bail to the closed position to stop the flow of line from the reel. In some spinning reels, the bail must be manually flipped back into the closed position, but many modern spinning reels allow you to firmly crank the reel one full rotation forward to automatically return the bail to the closed position.

Once the bail has returned to the closed position, as the reel is cranked forward the line will follow along the bail and find its way onto the roller, where it will stay as line is taken in.

Have your child get acquainted with using a spinning reel by practicing holding the line in the crease of the finger, flipping the bail open, releasing the line from the finger, and closing the bail. That will prepare your little fisherman for the process of casting fishing line with a spinning reel.

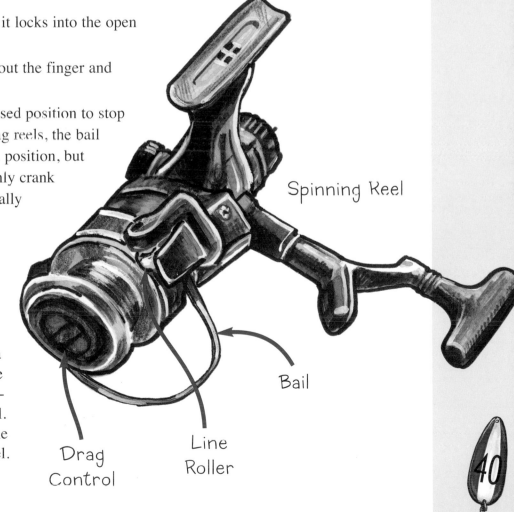

Spinning Reel

Bail

Line Roller

Drag Control

Spin-Casting Reels (Closed-Face)

1. Allow approximately one to two feet of line to hang from the tip of the rod to the sinker or bait. Remember not to reel your sinker or bait to the tip of the rod. Casting will be very difficult when the line is in this position. When the sinker or bait swings on a length of line from the rod tip, it acts like a pendulum when it is being cast, making for much longer and more accurate casts.

2. Depress the cast button on the rear of the reel and hold it down.

3. Raise the rod hand to shoulder level, keeping the button down. The rod is now ready to be cast.

4. Swing the rod forward, in the direction you wish your bait to land, releasing the button when the rod begins to point toward its intended target. Because getting the timing down takes some practice, I suggest trying this out before heading off on your adventure. Setting up a target, such as a hula hoop, for your child to aim at will help. However, fishing is not golf, and at this stage of the game you are just looking for general accuracy. Your child can start ten feet away from the intended target and slowly move outward as casting skills improve.

a. If the bait flies high in the air but comes down right in front of your child, your child is taking his or her thumb off the button too early in the cast.

b. If the bait slams down right in front of your child, the button is being released too late in the cast.

5. Once the cast is made, rotate the handle forward one full rotation to return the button to the lock, or fish-ready position.

Push cast button when starting cast.
Hold cast button down until rod is swung in intended direction of cast.

Spinning Reel (Open-Face)

1. (Same stuff, different reel) Allow approximately one to two feet of line to hang from the tip of the rod to the sinker or bait. Remember not to reel your sinker or bait to the tip of the rod. Casting will be very difficult when the line is in this position. When the sinker or bait swings on a length of line from the rod tip, it acts like a pendulum when it is being cast, making for much longer and more accurate casts.

2. Rotate the handle on the reel forward until the roller on the reel is immediately below the fishing pole. Some spinning reels will allow you to crank the reel backward, stopping automatically when the bail is in this position.

3. With the index (pointer) finger on the hand holding the rod, grab the line, landing it in the first crease of that finger. With little hands, your child may need to use the other hand to pull the line toward the pointer finger and place it in the first crease of that finger.

4. Flip the bail over so that it locks into the open position.

5. Raise the rod hand to shoulder level, holding the line in place. The rod is now ready to be cast.

6. Swing the rod forward, in the direction you wish your bait to land, releasing the line from your finger when the rod begins to point toward its intended target. Again, because getting the timing down takes some practice, I suggest trying this out before heading off on your adventure.

   a. If the bait flies high in the air but comes down right in front of your child, your child's finger is releasing the line too early in the cast.

   b. If the bait slams down right in front of your child, the line is being released too late in the cast.

7. Once the cast is made, the bail must be returned to its closed position to begin fishing or to take in the line.

Grab line with pointer finger.
Flip open the bail.
Hold line with finger until rod is swung in intended direction of cast.

Let the Adventure Begin!

Finally, Let's Go Fishing!!! First Things First

If you're in a place where you're looking for fish, then you're obviously by water, which means it's time to Put a Life Jacket on Your Child. It pays to invest in comfortably-fitting life jackets for children. You might want to let your child pick one out at the store to make sure it's comfortable so he or she does not resist the idea of wearing a life jacket on the adventure.

Assembling Your Fishing Rig

Here Fishy, Fishy

To find a good fishing spot, imagine that you are a fish. Wouldn't you likely hang out in a comfortable place with lots of good food?

If you're a fish, you're looking for something unique in the water, such as a change in color that may indicate a change in depth or a drop-off. You also like weeds, logs, stick piles, rocks, a sudden change in shoreline such as a point or sharp indentation, or water flowing into a lake as in a river mouth, creek, or drain. You may find other good areas under a dock or treefall, or in any water that offers shelter from the sunshine or the current in the water.

In fishermen's terms, this is all referred to as structure, or some place that would be inviting for a fish to hang out.

If you will be fishing in a river or stream, look for deeper pools in the river, commonly referred to as holes. These are most often found at bends in the river, on the opposite side of the direction of the bend. If the river is making a bend to the right, the pool will most commonly be found on the left side of the river bend. Also, fish downstream from large rocks or treefalls in the river; they provide a break in the current in which the fish can rest.

As you search for your spot, chat with your child about what you are looking for. That's the way new fishermen learn and can share in the sense of accomplishment once they catch a fish in a spot they helped pick out.

"Monkey See, Monkey Do"

Look around and see what other fishermen are using to catch fish. Take a page from your little adventurer's book and ask a lot of questions, specific questions (without being annoying, of course). Ask to see their rigs and how they have their lines set up. Believe me, subtle changes in your rig can make the difference in having just a good adventure or a really great one.

It's Knot Funny

At this point in the fishing adventure, you will have to tie a knot. A properly tied knot is vital to your child's success as a fisherman, as the vast majority of line breaks occur at the knot. Many knots, including the common overhand knot, can reduce the strength of fishing line by 50% or more. The lighter the weight of line you are using, the more crucial this becomes.

Spit and Knots

When you are tying knots on monofilament fishing line, a great amount of friction is created as the knot tightens. This friction generates heat that can significantly weaken the fishing line. Lubricating or moistening the line prior to drawing a knot tight will eliminate this issue. So, always moisten the fishing line before drawing the knot tight. This will reduce the friction caused by tightening your line. And yes, saliva works great for this purpose.

Fishermen come with a wonderful natural lubricant known as spit. Whenever you are tying a fishing knot, apply a small amount of this lubricant with your natural dispensers, your lips, and then snug the knot. Though you may think this is silly or even gross, most line breaks occur at the knot. Therefore, you'll want to make every effort to tie as strong a knot as possible, especially when you are working with lightweight lines. Always test your knot after tying to ensure its strength. A simple tug or two will tell you if you and your child will stay connected to the fish. An improperly tied knot will snap with minimal pressure.

The Palomar Knot

Learning several different knots is a good idea, as different knots serve different needs. However, if you're inclined to learn only one basic knot that will not require a sailor's training, then learn the Palomar knot.

This knot is very easy to tie and even your child can quickly become proficient at it with a bit of practice:

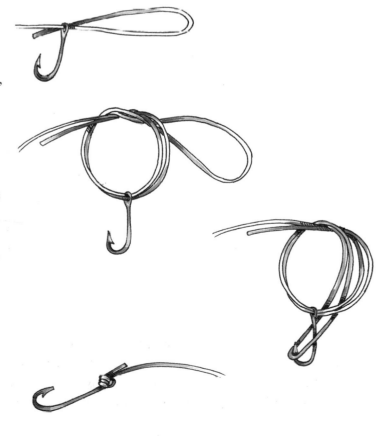

1. Double up the fishing line running through the eye of the hook or lure that you intend to tie. You can do this by pushing a loop of line through the eye or by running the line through the eye and then back through in the opposite direction.
2. Tie an overhand knot in the doubled line.
3. Pass the hook through the loop you created; moisten and snug the knot.
4. Trim the tag end within one-eighth inch of the knot.

44

Basic Fishing Rigs

Bottom-Fishing Rig 1

1. Tie a small hook directly to the fishing line.
2. Pinch one or two small split shots onto the fishing line, approximately eight to twelve inches from the hook.
3. Attach a worm, minnow, or other live bait to the hook.

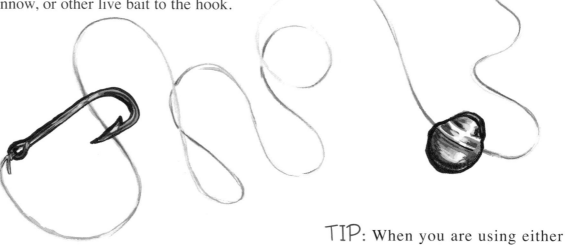

Bottom-Fishing Rig 2

1. Tie a snap swivel directly to your fishing line.
2. Open snap and attach a pre-tied hook or bait harness and small sinker to the snap; then close the snap.
3. Attach a worm, minnow, or other live bait to the hook.

TIP: When you are using either bottom-fishing rig, use just enough weight to do the job. Obviously, the deeper the water or the faster the water current, the more weight you will need.

Bobber-Fishing/Suspended Rig

1. Set up bottom-fishing rig 1, with split shot approximately eight inches from the hook.
2. Attach a stealth bobber to the line by sliding the rubber tubing or spring in an upward direction, exposing a groove in the bobber. Place the line through the groove and slide the rubber tubing or spring back to the original position.
3. Place the bobber far enough up on the line to keep the hook off the bottom.

Experiment with the depth adjustment of the bobber until you find the depth where the fish are holding.

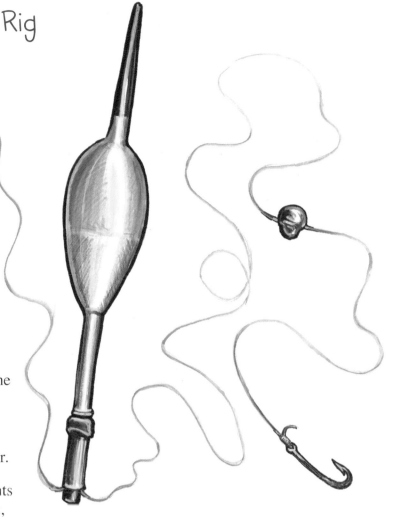

Finding the Bottom

When bobber fishing, the easiest way to determine the depth of the water is to start with the bobber several feet up from the split shots. Once you cast your line in the water, if the hook is resting on the bottom, the bobber will not stand upright in the water.

Continue to lower your bobber in small increments (six inches at a time) toward the hook after each cast, until the bobber stands straight in the water. This will indicate that your hook (or at least your split shots) is off the bottom. You can continue to lower your bobber toward the hook after each cast in order to further raise the hook off the bottom. Obviously, move the bobber in the opposite direction if you want to increase the depth of your bait. The target zone you are trying to accomplish in this method of fishing is to get your bait presented to the fish just above the bottom or just above the structure that you are fishing by (i.e., logs, stick pile, rocks, etc.). Oftentimes, this is the best way to present your bait, as a bottom-fishing rig may get snagged on such a structure or be below the fish. Also, the bobber acts as a strike indicator, which will help your child see when the fish is biting your bait.

Adjusting Weight

If you know your hook is off the bottom but the bobber continues to lie flat on the water, increase the size of the split shot on the line or add additional split shot so the weight on the line is sufficient to pull the bobber to an upright position on the surface of the water.

During this whole bobber-positioning process, if a fish hits your child's bait, you'll know you're in the zone! Leave the bobber where it is on the line and get ready for your child to catch some fish!

46

Hooking a Worm

Worms come in many different sizes, but they are all pretty much the same shape with similar colors. The head of the worm is the dark meat of the worm and, like a Thanksgiving turkey, is the least-favored meat. The tail section offers the white meat, most favored by the fish.

Night crawlers are among the largest and longest of bait worms. Red, or blood, worms (garden worms) are much smaller and often a better choice for pan fish. Since night crawlers can be more meat than a pan fish can handle, you might want to break the worm into smaller pieces so it does not intimidate the fish. A full night crawler might appear to a fish as a cow would appear to us; a portion of a night crawler would be more tempting and along the lines of a tasty steak to you and me.

When fishing with worms, at least when you first start fishing, try to keep things looking as natural as possible to the fish. Feed the hook through the worm starting near the tip/head of the worm, sliding the worm up the hook until it stops at the eye of the hook. Then push the hook through the body of the worm. By hooking the worm in this fashion, the worm will appear to hang naturally off the hook and not look bunched up into a worm wad. After all, when you see worms on the sidewalk on a rainy day, they are stretched out enjoying their swim in the puddle. You'd find it odd to see these worms gathered in bunches; so would a fish. However, there are times when the fish may continually steal/eat the worm off the hook when it is presented in this manner without actually getting hooked. In this case, you clearly have the fish's attention and it is interested in biting, so to hook such fish, you could bunch the worm onto the hook.

All worms are very sensitive to heat and will quickly die if the worm container is left in the sun. Always keep the container of worms in the shade or in a cooler. Unused worms can be kept lively for months if kept in your refrigerator in the container you purchased them in.

Hooking a Minnow

Minnows can be very hard to handle. They are lively, flippy little things and this is how we want them to appear when placed on the hook. I would strongly suggest the use of a minnow net, just to help you retrieve a minnow from your bait bucket. Without the aid of the net, just to get one in your hand can present a challenge. Once you do get one in your hand, there are two common methods of hooking the minnow.

Lip Hook: place the hook gently through the lips, beginning underneath the bottom lip and pushing the hook through the top lip. Try to avoid going through the minnow's head as this will immediately kill the minnow. But if you don't place the hook deep enough behind the lips, it may easily tear off the hook. You will quickly get the hang of this after hooking a few minnows.

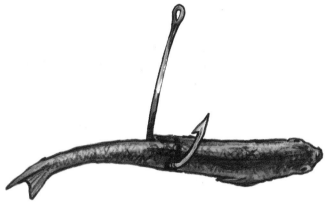

Dorsal Fin Hook: place the hook midway between the dorsal fin (the main fin on top of the minnow) and the tail fin, just below the top of the minnow. If you feed the hook too far down the middle of the fish's body, you will place the hook through the spine and this will paralyze the fish. Depending on the species of minnow you are using, many have a stripe running the side length of their body that acts as a good indicator of where their spine is located. Place the hook just above this line, behind the dorsal fin.

Both presentations, when hooked properly, will help the minnow to remain good and lively and more tempting to the fish you are pursuing.

Fresh lively minnows, more often than not, will catch you more fish than dead minnows. To keep your minnows lively, change the water in their bucket frequently while you are fishing or keep them in a minnow bucket in the water where you are fishing to allow fresh water to flow through the bucket. There will be times when the fish will go gaa gaa over just about any bait or minnow that is presented to them, including dead minnows. So should you find yourself out of live bait, don't hesitate to use the floaters in your bucket as the fish may still be interested in them as well.

Casting Line upon the Waters

Frequent Flier Miles

Children love to endlessly reel in their lines and cast them out again. However, keeping a line forever flying in the air greatly diminishes the chance of catching fish. Eventually, your little adventurer must learn that the bait needs to be in the water in order to catch fish! You may try telling children that the rod has only so many casts in it and if they use them all up, they will no longer be able to fish.

Hunting and Fishing

Oftentimes, when you first begin your day of fishing, you will have to hunt around to find where the fish are hanging out. In your child's defense, varying the location of their casts allows them to cover a lot of territory and find where the fish are located. You and your child should seek new water if the fish have not opted to at least nibble at your offering within twenty to thirty minutes. Don't waste the day fishing in just one area of the water if the fish are not present or biting. Vary where you fish and where you cast your line until you find the fish. Also, change around from a bottom fishing rig to a bobber/suspended fishing rig while looking for fish. This frequent change will also help keep your child interested in catching the fish.

Stay in the Suburbs

When fishing around a structure, have your child cast just outside the structure in the "suburbs," and not "downtown" in the middle of it. In other words, cast just outside the weedbed or the stick pile. While fish stay within the comfort and safety of the structure to avoid becoming a larger fish's entrée, they will look for food by venturing just outside the structure.

Snags

Suburban fishing also helps avoid snagging lines in or on the structure you are fishing. Snags are to fishing what falling is to riding a bike: they're part of the learning curve. No matter how good we get, they're still bound to happen. Snags keep us humble.

When your child casts into a snag (notice, I said "when" and not "if"), do not scold, as this can happen to any of us. Whether the obstruction can be seen above the water or the line has been pulled into countless foulings hidden underneath the surface, remember: one quick retie and the problem is solved.

Your child may snag the same submerged structure, such as a log, repeatedly. If so, instruct your child to avoid casting into that area, so that both of you can get back to fishing and you can stop retying hooks. If you're getting that much pleasure out of retying the line, you must get my other book, *Adventures in Quilting!*

Getting out of a Jam

Once your child has pulled into a snag, you can try several things that may save the bait from certain ill-fate. In any of these attempts to free the snag, do not exert too much pressure on the rod. Both rod and reel have breaking points, and nothing will bring an enjoyable fishing adventure to a close quicker than broken equipment.

First, pull back on the rod to see if the snag seems to be giving way. The hook may just be on weeds or debris that can be reeled in with a little extra effort. If you reel in debris, please do not throw it back into the water after releasing the hook. Please dispose of it properly so that this does not occur to someone else.

If you are not fortunate enough for the simple fix, try a couple of sharp upward or side-to-side thrusts on the rod to free the line. If this does not do the trick, try attacking the snag from a couple of different angles. To do this, release the pressure on the line by depressing the cast button or opening the bail on the reel. With the fishing rod in hand, take several steps down shore or move to another area of the boat. Tighten the line and apply pressure on the line away from the snag. If this does not work, simply move in the opposite direction on the shore or in the boat and repeat the process.

If you're fishing in water with a strong current or one with a lot of rocks, you may have luck just letting the line go slack and allowing the current to work for you. In a rocky area, hooks will have a tendency to lodge between the rocks, but the current may pull the hook free of the snag once you allow some slack in the line.

If the angles don't work, you can shake the daylights out of the rod. However, if the snag does not quickly free itself, then all the shaking in the world will only set the hook deeper into the snag. You can then kiss this rig goodbye.

Breaking the Line

When all else fails and the line must be broken, there are right and wrong ways to do this as well. Reel the line so that it is taut. Then, on a closed-face reel, tighten down the drag so as not to allow any line to release from the reel. Point the rod directly at the snag and walk or pull the rod directly away from the snag, all the while keeping the rod pointing straight at the snag. This will put all of the pressure on the line and not the rod or reel, eventually causing the line to snap. If you are using a spinning reel, hold firmly onto the spool to stop the line from coming off the reel, and then pull the rod away from the snag in the same fashion.

WARNING: Do not wrap the fishing line around your fingers or hands to free the snag. Monofilament fishing line, when pulled taut, becomes very thin and very sharp, quickly providing a painfully deep cut. (This is experience talking, believe me!)

Then, as we say in the fishing world, "If at first you don't succeed, tie, tie again." Okay, we don't really say that, but how many positive sayings are there related to fishing snags?

As a result of a snag, or if you are fishing in areas with lots of structure, your line may become frayed or feel rough to the touch when you slide it through your fingers. After each snag or occasionally throughout your fishing adventure, run the first few feet of line up from the hook through your fingertips. The line should feel very smooth to the touch. If it feels or appears rough, this is a weak spot in the line and should be retied above the frayed area of the line. Otherwise, virtually any tension on the line will cause it to break.

Catching a Fish!

Getting Bites and Keeping Them Interested

Fish bites feel like sharp tugs at the end of the fishing line. Depending on the species, size, and feeding patterns of fish, you may feel one hard, sharp tug; a series of small tugs; or a slow, gentle pull on the end of your line. If you are using a bobber, you may not feel the fish bite at all. Instead, you will see the bobber bounce on top of the water or disappear below the surface. If the fish stops biting, try to keep it interested; slowly reel in the line or pull back the rod a few feet and then stop. Often, the slight movement of the bait will entice the fish to hit again, thinking its meal may be about to leave.

At times, the only way you may get fish to bite is to continue to move your bait through the water. During these times, once you cast your line, continue to retrieve the line very, very slowly, providing subtle movement to your bait. You may find the fish will only hit when the bait is moving.

I cannot emphasize enough that CHANGE is a very successful part of fishing. Try many different offerings, no matter how slight or aggressive, until you find what the fish are interested in biting. You may have to change your setup or your whole presentation many times during your adventure as fish can be very finicky and vary their desires throughout the time that you are fishing. CHANGE IS GOOD. Once you discover what they like, stick with it until they change their minds again.

Setting the Hook

Sometimes, fish will work with you and hook themselves when they bite the hook. More often, to stick the hook into the fish's mouth, you or your child will have to quickly pull back on the rod while the fish is biting. This is referred to as setting the hook. Hard to believe, with hooks as sharp as they are, that fish are not solidly hooked at the slightest contact with the point of the hook. However, if your child does not get into the habit of setting the hook when a fish bites, more fish will tend to get away than make it to the trophy photo shoot.

While your child is fishing, have him or her hold the rod parallel to the water or thereabouts. This position will best allow your child to feel a bite, see the rod react to a bite, and allow enough room to pull the rod back and set the hook when the fish does bite.

Keeping a Tight Line

As the fish is being reeled in, keeping the fishing line tight right up through the landing of the fish is very important. Your child can easily achieve this by keeping the rod tip pointed in a slight upward direction while reeling in the fish, allowing the rod to bend and keep pressure on the line. The purpose of a tight line is to keep pressure on the hook in the fish's mouth. If your child allows slack in the line while reeling in the fish, the fish may, with a quick head shake, find its freedom. This we refer to as spitting the hook. And just for your information, fish really can spit!

Holy Cow, We Hooked a Monster!

Since large fish like to feed on smaller fish, including pan fish, a big one could show up when you least expect it. So here are a few words of wisdom to help land that big fish: DON'T FREAK OUT! This is pure excitement, and you and your child's reaction will be priceless when shared together.

Immediately upon being hooked, a large fish may pull a lot of line from the reel. This running is okay and part of the fun. When the fish is pulling the line from the reel, have your child stop turning the reel handle until the fish stops pulling out the line. Do not reel in the line until the fish seems to be tiring and you can actually take in line onto the reel when you turn the handle.

Larger fish are quite powerful and may choose to just sit at the bottom, not allowing your child to take any line in on them. If fishermen continue to reel when the fish is pulling out line or when they cannot take in any line, the fishing line will develop a serious case of the twists that will not only weaken the line but also make it very difficult to cast, as it will develop the tendency to coil around the rod or loop up on itself when slack.

Once the fish stops to take a break, your child should slowly pull up and back on the rod, then quickly lower the rod toward the fish, reeling in the line as the rod tip lowers. This pumping the rod should be repeated until the fish is brought in to land. A large fish may make several runs while it is being brought in, or it may jump out of the water quite a bit. Again, this is all part of the fun. You and your child are going to be very excited, but do not rush landing the fish. If you're pan fishing, you're using lighter fishing line, and too much pressure on the line will cause it to break. So just be patient, keep a tight line, and the fish will be yours.

If, during the battle of the big fish, the line continues to pull too freely from the reel, then slowly tighten the drag to apply more tension to the line. If it appears that the fish is pulling the rod from your child's hand and the line is not pulling from the reel, quickly loosen the drag to relieve pressure on the line. You may have to adjust the drag a few times in the course of landing a large fish.

Just be careful not to over-tighten the drag, as it may cause the line to snap. And if the line snaps because of something that you did to lose your child's big fish, you'd better be able to catch another one immediately, just as big or bigger, or your name is mud!

Landing the Fish

Now that you've brought the fish close to shore or the boat, you need to land it. Most pan fish can be landed by simply lifting up the rod and pulling the fish out of the water. Larger fish will need to be landed with a net. The fish will show that it's ready to be landed when it allows itself to be pulled to the surface of the water or gently rolls on its side just below the surface of the water.

If a fish keeps its head down and continues to pull hard on the line, it's just not ready to come in yet. Let your child enjoy the excitement of fighting the fish and do not attempt to land the fish until it has been tired out. When you decide to net the fish, have your child pull up on the rod, lifting the fish's head toward the surface of the water.

Always net the fish head first, not the other way around. Fish can only swim forward, so trying to net a fish from the back will usually result in an embarrassing chase that is most always won by the fish.

Handling the Fish

Getting a Good Grip

Wet your hands before handling the fish so you don't remove the protective layer of slime on its outside.

When holding smaller fish, grab the fish from the bottom, just behind the gills, and avoid placing your hand over the dorsal fin on top of the fish's back, as it has sharp spines that can offer quite a poke.

When handling larger fish, slip a finger inside the gill, just inside the gill plate (the outside cheek of the fish) and slide your finger towards the mouth opening until it stops. Be careful not to grab onto the red gills inside the gill plate as they will easily tear, causing the fish to bleed out and perish.

If you have landed a large toothy fish such as a pike, you may want to avoid placing your finger in its gills to avoid having your finger slide up into its mouth. For these fish, grab them from the top, just behind their gills, and hold onto them firmly, but not too tight. This will not harm the fish or your fingers and will allow you to easily handle the fish for hook removal.

Removing the Hook

Once you are securely holding the fish, grab the top of the hook where it meets the line and push down on the hook to release it from the fish's mouth. This may take some pressure on your part if the barb of the hook is buried deep in the fish's mouth. To help free the hook, apply a back-and-forth twisting motion as you press down on it. If you cannot reach the hook with your fingers, use needle-nose pliers, hemostats, or a hook remover to get ahold of the hook and remove it.

Release It?

Consider releasing any fish you do not intend to eat. This will help to keep the population strong for other fishermen to enjoy. When releasing the fish, gently place it in the water with your hand and hold on until it swims free from your hand. Slowly moving the fish forward and backward in the water will help flush water through the fish's gills and aid in reviving it. If you intend to release the fish your child is catching, try not to keep it out of the water for a long time, as the fish will suffocate and not survive its return to the water. If the fish is severely wounded from the hook removal, returning it to the water makes no sense, especially if the hook remains in the fish. Other fish, birds, or animals may die by eating the fish with the hook in it.

Keep It?

For any fish you plan to keep, a fish basket works great to hold fish in the water and still keep them fresh and alive while you continue to fish.

If you're keeping larger fish, use a stringer by poking the point of the stringer upward through the bottom jaw, out of the fish's mouth, and back through the ring at the opposite end of the stringer. Additional fish can be added to the stringer by poking the stringer up through the jaw, out of the fish's mouth, and allowing the fish to slide down the stringer to the first fish. Do not feed the stringer through the fish's gills, as this will tear the gills and cause the fish to bleed out and perish.

Tie a stringer or fish basket securely to a solid object on shore or on the boat. Many a fisherman has had a successful day ruined when the catch made a getaway, stringer and all (again, personal experience confirms this). This aside, the fish attached to the stringer or in a fish basket that has come free will perish needlessly.

Preserving the Moment

It's Picture Time!

Be sure to bring along a camera on your adventure, and try to get a close-up of your child and the fish. The best part of the picture will be the expression on your child's face, so make sure this is the focus of the picture. Also, in a separate photo, try to capture some of the background of the area where your child caught the fish.

Taking the picture of the fish right when it has been caught is very important, as dead fish quickly lose their coloration. Pictures taken several hours later with a stiff colorless fish are much less appealing. As well, you will want to capture your child's emotions when they are at their peak, which is right when your child has landed the fish.

Time marches on, and with it goes the vividness of our memories. Pictures are a great reminder of past events, but most of the treasures of the experience lie in the small details, which tend to fade with time. Enter the fishing journal.

Your Fishing Journal

In a journal, jot down the dates, locations, and people involved in the event, as well as any occurrences that helped to make the outing memorable. Some of the greatest memories of your outings will not be about the great catches but about the simple things that happened on your adventure. The sighting of certain wildlife or funny things said or done can be great reminders of days gone by.

The fishing journal can also help you and your child catch more fish in the future. In your entries, include information on weather, exact location, what baits worked if you caught fish, and what baits did not. A brief review of past adventures can quickly bring to mind the formula you used to catch fish on one of your prior outings. Also, if others were having success in your area and you did not, ask them questions and record what to use to make your next adventure more successful.

Fishing: A Sport for All Seasons

Contrary to popular belief, fishing is not just a summer sport. Great, child-friendly fishing is possible the entire year round. In northern states, ice fishing is a great family sport and can be experienced with minimal investment. Fall fishing can be very productive as large schools of fish congregate by shore near river mouths as they prepare to spawn. Many species of fish, in preparation for their winter survival, also will feed more aggressively as the water cools.

Springtime brings the spawning of different species of fish and can again mean excellent near-shore fishing, where fish may continue to hang out until the weather warms the water with the approach of summer. Also, after spending the winter months cooped up in your house, you'll enjoy getting outdoors to spend some time with your children. If you reside in southern or coastal states, the winter season provides cooler, more comfortable fishing conditions, and this means more patience for both you and your children.

Promote the Sport

For lots of reasons, many children today do not have the opportunity to experience the outdoors. If you have the chance to take a child fishing, please do so. The experience will be most gratifying for you and may be a lifelong gift for that child.

My family and I hope the Adventures with Jonny series will open the minds of as many children and adults as possible to the wonderful experiences that await them in the great outdoors.

Adventure Checklist

- ☐ Fishing Pole
- ☐ Tackle Box and Tackle
- ☐ Little Bandages (just in case)
- ☐ Minnow Bucket and Minnow Net
- ☐ Stringer or Fish Basket
- ☐ Landing Net
- ☐ Hook Remover, Hemostats, or Needle Nose Pliers
- ☐ Bait
- ☐ Camera

- ☐ Snacks and Drinks
- ☐ Cooler (for fish's return trip to your house)
- ☐ Foul-Weather Gear or Rain Jacket (if weather gets bad)
- ☐ Suntan Lotion (if weather is good)
- ☐ Bug Repellent
- ☐ Chairs
- ☐ LIFE JACKET FOR EACH LITTLE ADVENTURER
- ☐ PATIENCE FOR EACH LITTLE ADVENTURER'S INSTRUCTOR

NAME THAT FISH!
Family Game

NAME THAT FISH is a fun game designed to help children identify the various species of popular fresh-water game fish and learn about their preferred habitats, diets, and baits of choice. This is a great game to be played in between bites while fishing or as an enticer between much-anticipated fishing adventures.

To play, first read the clues for each fish to your child and point out the identifying clues as illustrated in the picture of each fish. Then read back the clues to your child (naturally with them not looking at the pictures) and see how many clues it takes before they can **NAME THAT FISH!**

Once they have been through the game a few times, pick a fish and ask your child how many clues they can recite back to you from memory. You will be surprised at how quickly they catch on and will be able to identify their fish.

BLUEGILL

My name is how you know me.

My Munchies

Small Minnows

Garden Worms

Crickets

My Hangouts

Weedy Beds

Sticky Piles

Ponds

The Biggest Ever

4 POUNDS

1/3 POUND ······› Average Size

How to Catch Me!

Fishermen catch bluegill by using small garden worms or small minnows fished below a bobber so that the bait hangs above the bottom of the water. You can also try casting a very small spinner and slowly reeling it in.

Short body that is very narrow near tail

Light green color, faded stripes from top to bottom

Tail is slightly forked

Blue spot on tip of gill, orange patch below chin

ROCKBASS

My name is where you will find me.

My Munchies

Small Minnows

Garden Worms

Crickets

My Hangouts

Rocky Bottoms

Weedy Beds

Sticky Piles

The Biggest Ever

3 POUNDS

1/3 POUND ···· Average Size

How to Catch Me!

Fishermen catch rockbass by using a very small jig, baited with a small minnow, garden worm, or small rubber grub. Slowly bouncing the jig off the bottom and stopping once in a while seems to work best.

Many rows of small black dots from head to tail

Dark patches across the side

Dark spot on gill

Greenish brown body

58

CRAPPIE

Just a fish, not a bad word.

My Munchies

Small Minnows

Small Crayfish

Crickets

My Hangouts

Weedy Beds

Sunken Logs

Sticky Piles

The Biggest Ever

5 POUNDS

1/3 POUND ·····Average Size

How to Catch Me!

Fishermen catch crappie by using their favorite bait, small minnows, fished below a bobber so they hang off the bottom. You can also try using a small jig baited with a small white or yellow rubber grub bounced slowly off the bottom.

Short body with narrow tail, little forking

Small head but bigger mouth than bluegill

Dark patches or stripes on body and fins

Greenish brown or yellowish brown body

59

NORTHERN PIKE

Long, toothy, and slimy is what I am all about.

My Munchies

Big minnows, suckers, or any fish smaller than them

My Hangouts

Weedy Beds | Lily Pads | Sunken Logs

The Biggest Ever

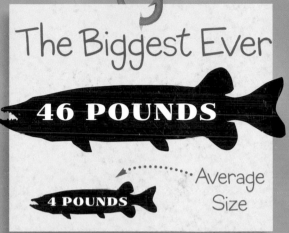

46 POUNDS

4 POUNDS

Average Size

How to Catch Me!

Fishermen catch northern pike by using large minnows or suckers fished below a bobber. It's best if you can fish your bait just above a weedy bed or right alongside a weedy bed or patch of lily pads. You can also cast large red and white spoons or spinners and quickly reel them in.

Fin on back located near tail fin

Long skinny body

Big sharp teeth

Greenish body with white spots, fins tipped with orange

WALLEYE

Big eyes help me see well at night.

My Munchies

Minnows   Leeches

Night Crawlers

My Hangouts

Rocky   Gravelly   Weedy
Bottoms   Bottoms   Beds

The Biggest Ever

20 POUNDS

2 POUNDS → Average Size

How to Catch Me!

Fishermen catch walleyes using night crawlers fished on a crawler harness near the bottom. You can also try using a leech fished below a bobber, just off the bottom, or bait a medium-sized jig with a leech and slowly bounce it off the bottom.

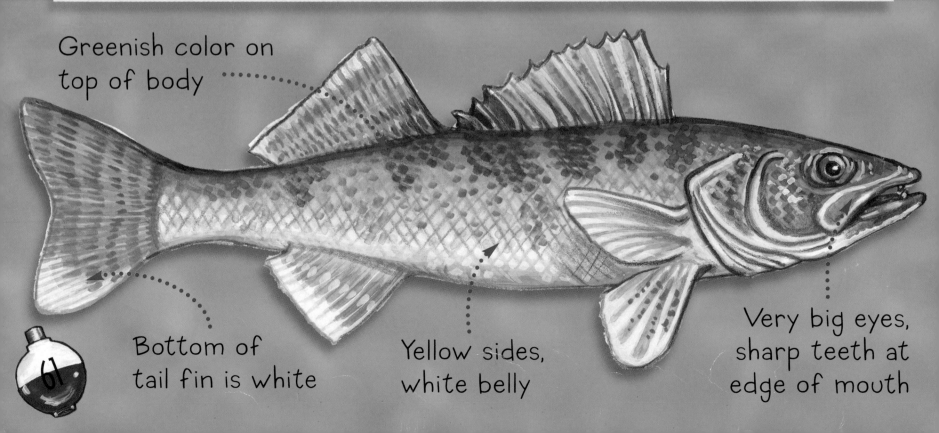

Greenish color on top of body

Bottom of tail fin is white

Yellow sides, white belly

Very big eyes, sharp teeth at edge of mouth

61

YELLOW PERCH

Great taste in a less filling fish.

My Munchies

Small
Minnows

Garden
Worms

Crayfish

My Hangouts

Weedy
Beds

Drop-
offs

Sticky
Piles

The Biggest Ever

4 POUNDS

1/3 POUND Average Size

How to Catch Me!

Fishermen catch yellow perch using "perch spreaders" baited with small minnows, fished at the bottom of the water. A perch spreader is a two-hook assembly that allows you to catch two perch at a time. It's best to try fishing on the deep side of a drop-off for perch.

Six or more wide dark stripes running from top to bottom

Short narrow body

Greenish body

Yellow belly, orange fins

LARGE MOUTH BASS

Big mouth, big game.

My Munchies

Large
Minnows

Frogs

Crayfish

My Hangouts

Weedy
Beds

Lily
Pads

Sunken
Logs

The Biggest Ever

20 POUNDS

1 POUND

Average
Size

How to Catch Me!

Fishermen catch large mouth bass using large rubber worms bounced off the bottom of the water. You can also try casting lures that float on the top of the water and reeling them in near lily pads or weedy beds.

Greenish body

Hinge of jaw runs below
or behind eye

Line of dark
circles running from gill to tail

SMALL MOUTH BASS

Small mouth, tough fighter.

My Munchies

Crayfish

Worms

Minnows

My Hangouts

Large Rocky Bottoms

Weedy Beds

Sticky Piles

The Biggest Ever

12 POUNDS

1 POUND   Average Size

How to Catch Me!

Fishermen catch small mouth bass with minnows or night crawlers fished on the bottom and slowly turning the reel so the bait moves across the bottom of the water. You can also try a spinner, spoons, or floating lures. Cast any lure near weeds, rocks, or sticks and slowly reel it in.

Greenish body, 3 dark stripes on gill

Reddish colored eye

Patchy dark stripes from top to bottom

Hinge of jaw stops before eye

CRAYFISH

Not a fish at all, as I look like a lobster.

My Munchies

Dead Fish or Minnows

My Hangouts

Under Rocks   Under Logs   Under Docks

The Biggest Ever

6 INCHES

2 INCHES

Average Size

How to Catch Me!

Fishermen don't actually try to catch crayfish with a fishing rod. Instead they set traps to catch crayfish during the night so they can use them for bait in the morning, or you can buy crayfish for bait at many bait stores.

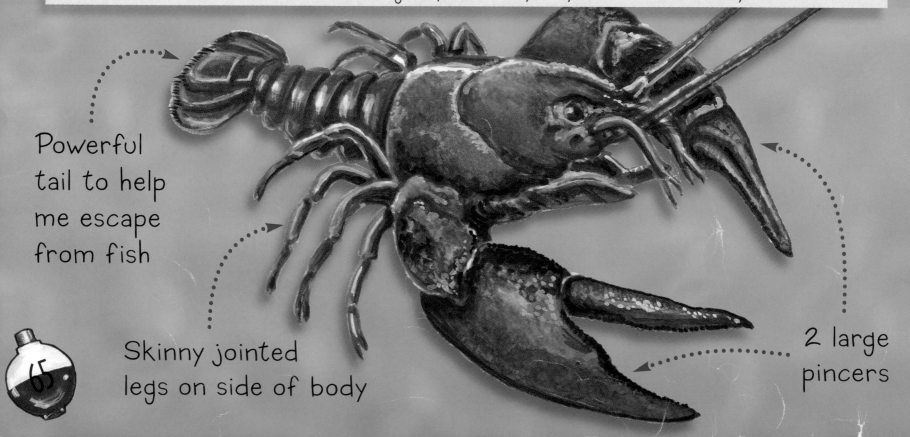

Powerful tail to help me escape from fish

Skinny jointed legs on side of body

2 large pincers

CATFISH

The only fish with whiskers.

My Munchies

Worms

Crayfish

Minnows

My Hangouts

Muddy Bottoms   Deep pools in rivers

The Biggest Ever

50 POUNDS

1 POUND   Average Size

How to Catch Me!

Fishermen catch catfish with dough balls fished on the bottom. You can also try using worms fished right on the bottom. No matter what you decide to use to fish for catfish, fish it at the bottom of the water.

Grayish or brownish colored body

Sharp spines in dorsal and pectoral fins

Whiskers around mouth

66

My Fishing Journal

Date ....

I was at ....

I was with ....

I caught ....

....

I used ....

Date ....

I was at ....

I was with ....

I caught ....

....

I used ....

Date ....

I was at ....

I was with ....

I caught ....

....

I used ....

Date ....

I was at ....

I was with ....

I caught ....

....

I used ....

Date ....

I was at ....

I was with ....

I caught ....

....

I used ....

Date ....

I was at ....

I was with ....

I caught ....

....

I used ....

Date ....

I was at ....

I was with ....

I caught ....

....

I used ....

Date ....

I was at ....

I was with ....

I caught ....

....

I used ....

My Fishing Journal

Date ....

I was at ....

I was with ....

I caught ....

....

I used ....

Date ....

I was at ....

I was with ....

I caught ....

....

I used ....

Date ....

I was at ....

I was with ....

I caught ....

....

I used ....

Date ....

I was at ....

I was with ....

I caught ....

....

I used ....

Date ....

I was at ....

I was with ....

I caught ....

....

I used ....

Date ....

I was at ....

I was with ....

I caught ....

....

I used ....

Date ....

I was at ....

I was with ....

I caught ....

....

I used ....

Date ....

I was at ....

I was with ....

I caught ....

....

I used ....

About the Author

Michael DiLorenzo, a married father of three and a passionate fan of his home state of Michigan and its Upper Peninsula, has logged countless hours fishing the state's abundant rivers and lakes. Like his father before him, he, too, introduced his children to fishing at a young age and has towed them around through all four seasons of fishing in Michigan. At the writing of this book, with his son, Jon, just eight years old, he looks forward to the many adventures that await them together in the outdoors.

About Running Moose Publications

Running Moose Publications, the producer of the Adventures with Jonny series, intends to release a steady stream of adventure books, each taking Jonny on a different outdoor quest that can be enjoyed by children and their families. The books will continue to open with a children's story to pique your child's interest in the activity and will then be followed by a "how-to" section to help you introduce your child to the featured activity. The next publication in this series, *Adventures with Jonny, Ice Fishing! The Coolest Sport on Earth*, is slated for release in October 2006.

Future books will include adventures about camping/backpacking, canoeing/kayaking, archery, and hunting. Our aim is for the series to have the momentum of a running moose. After all, how do you stop a running moose …?

About the Illustrator

As a girl, Jenniffer Julich loved to draw. Her artistic mother would often bring her and her twin sister on outdoor sketching adventures. Her mother often commented, "I do not know if there is an art career for the tiny little pictures you draw, Jenniffer." Years later, when Jenniffer graduated from the classical animation program at Sheridan College in Oakville, Ontario, she found her calling in storyboarding, which is drawing hundreds of tiny little pictures to visualize scripts and stories. After college, she became a storyboarder for film and television, working in Toronto.

Jenniffer is married, has two children, and began her own production company in St. Catharines, Ontario. As principal artist of Jnnffr Productions (www.jnnffr.com), she has art-directed films/video (tiny pictures), created murals (giant pictures), and has illustrated numerous books (colored pictures). When her kids were younger, some of her family's outdoor adventures included snake catching, frogging, and crabbing. Now that her kids are teens, her family is involved in 1750's fort reenactments and agritourism adventures.